new loftspace design

El loft que conocemos hoy en día difiere bastante de su concepción original, que generó un tipo de viviendas popularizadas a partir de 1960 en ciudades como Londres, Berlín y Nueva York. Por entonces se trataban de verdaderas fábricas reconvertidas en el hogar de artistas con escasos recursos. En la actualidad, entendemos un loft como una vivienda de planta libre, diáfana y flexible que alude a lo industrial a partir de materiales como el hierro o la madera a la vista. Los nuevos materiales y las innovadoras técnicas de diseño han originado una nueva generación de lofts, donde destaca su alto grado de sofisticación convirtiéndose en un estilo de vida anhelado por muchos. Las viviendas que aparecen en este libro evidencian esta nueva tendencia en donde encontramos las más variadas soluciones de diseño para resolver el loft contemporáneo.

Le Loft que nous connaissons aujourd'hui diffère assez de sa conception initiale qui a produit ce type de logements, popularisés à partir des années 60 dans des villes comme Londres, Berlin et New York. Il s'agissait alors de véritables usines reconverties en logement d'artistes avec de faibles moyens. Aujourd'hui nous concevons un loft comme un espace ouvert, diaphane et flexible qui évoque ce qui est industriel à partir de matériaux à vue comme le fer ou le bois. Les nouveaux matériaux et techniques de design ont engendré une nouvelle génération de lofts caractérisés par un haut niveau de sophistication devenant un style de vie recherché par beaucoup. Ce choix fait ressortir cette nouvelle tendance où l'on trouve les solutions de design les plus variées pour transformer le loft contemporain.

Il Loft che si conosce oggigiorno è piuttosto differente dal tipo di alloggio che la corrente originale rese famoso, a partire dagli anni 60, in città come Londra, Berlino e New York. In quel tempo si trattava di vere fabbriche, ristrutturate con pochi mezzi e adattate a residenze per artisti. Attualmente per Loft ci riferiamo ad un alloggio con una pianta libera, trasparente e flessibile che allude all'industria per i materiali utilizzati, come il ferro o il legno, che vengono lasciati in vista. I nuovi materiali e le tecniche di progettazione hanno dato origine a una nuova generazione di Lofts dove emerge un alto grado di raffinatezza che lo ha trasformato in uno stile di vita desiderato da molti. La selezione che presentiamo mette in evidenza questa nuova tendenza e offre le più svariate soluzioni di progettazione per risolvere il Loft contemporaneo.

Ein Loft von heute unterscheidet sich von der Grundidee der sechziger Jahre, als es in London, Berlin, New York und anderen Großstädten populär wurde, ehemalige Fabriketagen ohne allzu viel Aufwand in Atelierwohnungen zu verwandeln. Heute versteht man unter einem Loft eine Wohnung mit einem offenen, flexiblem Grundriss. Metall und Holzoberflächen erinnern an den industriellen Ursprung der Idee. Neue Materialien und Designtechniken haben eine neue Generation von Lofts hervorgebracht, die sich durch ihre ausgeklügelte, durchdachte Gestaltung auszeichnen und für einen immer beliebter werdenden Lebensstil stehen. Die hier vorliegende Auswahl bestätigt diese innovative Tendenz und bezeugt, dass es bei den zeitgenössischen Lofts die vielfältigsten gestalterischen Lösungen gibt.

The loft as we know it today is quite different from its original conception during the 1960s, when this typology of residence became popularized in cities like London, Berlin and New York. At that time, lofts were indeed reconverted warehouses that artists maintained with very few means. Today a loft can simply imply an open-plan, diaphanous and flexible space that alludes to an industrial aesthetic through exposed materials like steel and wood. New materials and design techniques have produced a new generation of lofts that have transformed it into a sophisticated asset desired by many. This selection bears proof of this growing trend, offering a wide variety of design solutions for today's contemporary loft.

Baratloo-Balch Architects | New York, USA
Friedrich Loft
New York, USA | 2000

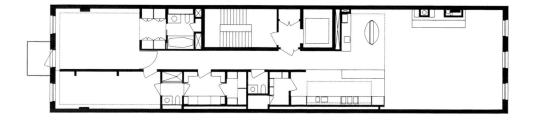

Cha & Innerhofer Architecture + Design | New York, USA

Lehman Loft
New York, USA | 2003

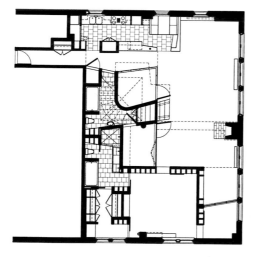

Chelsea Atelier | New York, USA

Carol Austin Loft
New York, USA | 2004

Delphine Ammann | London, UK
Ammann Loft
Frauenfeld, Switzerland | 2001

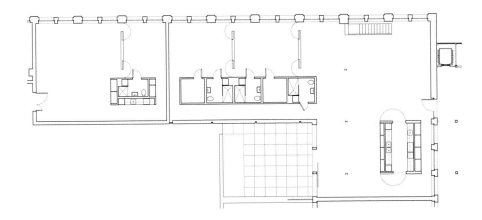

Frederick Fisher and Partners Architects | Los Angeles, USA
Hampton Court
Venice, USA | 2003

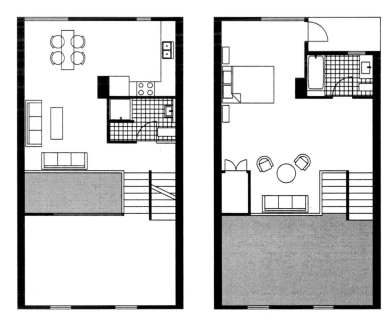

Frederick Fisher and Partners Architects | Los Angeles, USA
Venice Court
Venice, USA | 2003

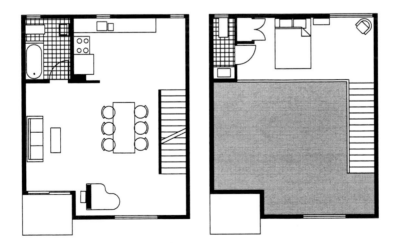

Gerrard + Tan Architects | New York, USA
Brownhill Residence
New York, USA | 2002

Gert van den Keuken | Paris, France
Loft in Montparnasse
Paris, France | 2000

Gluckman Mayner Architects | New York, USA
Tribeca Loft
New York, USA | 2003

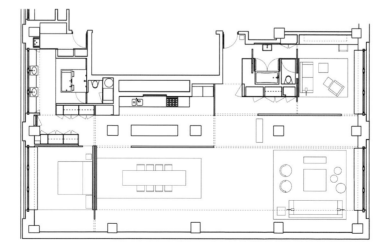

HanrahanMeyers Architects | New York, USA
Glasser Loft
New York, USA | 2003

Ignacio Cardenal | Barcelona, Spain
Loft St. J. Malta
Barcelona, Spain | 2001

James Wagman | New York, USA
Sharp + Gilpin Loft
New York, USA | 2000

John Martin / Four Ten Architects | London, UK
Mc. Donough Loft
London, UK | 2000

Maria Vives, Lluís Escarmis / GCA Arquitectes | Barcelona, Spain
Loft in the Old City
Barcelona, Spain | 2002

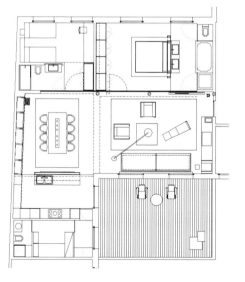

Mario Connío | Buenos Aires, Argentina
Terrace Loft
Buenos Aires, Argentina | 2000

Mark Grzegorczyk / MG Architects | London, UK
St. John Street Loft
London, UK | 2003

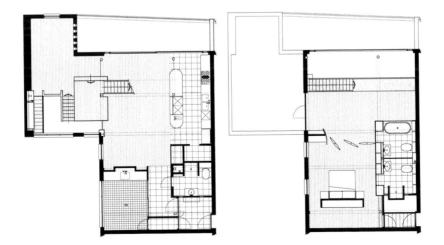

Ogawa / Depardon Architects | New York, USA
Greenwich Village Loft
New York, USA | 2004

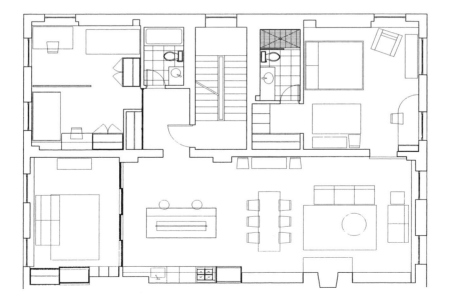

Ruhl Walker Architects | Boston, USA
H / R Loft
Boston, USA | 2000

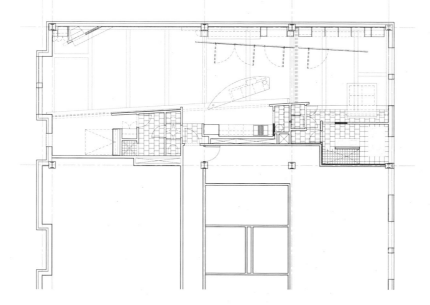

Sarah Folch Estudi d'Interiorisme | Barcelona, Spain
Textile Factory
Barcelona, Spain | 2002

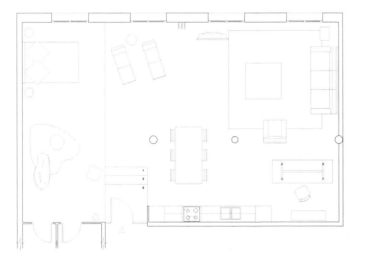

Sergio Sessa | Buenos Aires, Argentina
Loft in Buenos Aires
Buenos Aires, Argentina | 2000

Victoria Blau Architect | New York, USA
Duane Street Loft
New York, USA | 2002

Victoria Blau Architect | New York, USA
Thirty Crosby Street Loft
New York, USA | 2002

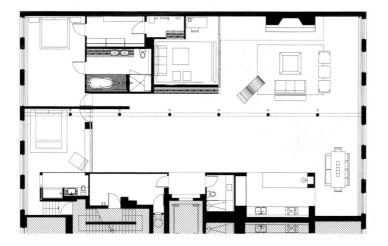

Xavière Bouyer | Paris, France
Loft in Pigalle
Paris, France | 2000

Baratloo-Balch Architects
155 West 88th Street, New York,
NY 10024, USA
P +1 212 873 6450
cb155w88@netscape.net
Friedrich Loft - Photos: © Jordi Miralles

Cha & Innerhofer Architecture + Design
611 Broadway 540, New York, NY, USA
P +1 212 477 6957
F +1 212 353 3286
www.cha-innerhofer.com
Lehman Loft - Photos: © Dao Lou Zha

Chelsea Atelier
245 7th Avenue, Suite 6, New York, NY 10001, USA
P +1 212 255 3494
F +1 212 255 3495
ayhan@chelseaatelier.com
Carol Austin Loft - Photos: © Bjorg Photography

Delphine Ammann
Frauenfeld, Switzerland
Ammann Loft - Photos: © Reto Guntli / Zapaimages

Frederick Fisher and Partners Architects
12248 Santa Monica Blvd, Los Angeles, CA 90025, USA
P +1 310 820 6680
F +1 310 820 6118
www.fisherpartners.net
Hampton Court - Photos: © Undine Pröhl
Venice Court - Photos: © Undine Pröhl

Gerrard + Tan Architects
145 Hudson Street, New York, NY 10013, USA
P +1 212 226 1910
F +1 212 226 6041
info@gerrardtan.com
Brownhill Residence - Photos: © David Joseph

Gert van den Keuken
Paris, France
Loft in Montparnasse - Photos: © Ricardo Labougle,
Ana Cardinale

Gluckman Mayner Architects
250 Hudson Street, New York, NY 10013, USA
P +1 212 929 0100
F +1 212 929 0833
info@gluckmanmayner.com
www.gluckmanmayner.com
Tribeca Loft - Photos: © Harry Zernike

HanrahanMeyers Architects
135 West 20th Street, Suite 300, New York,
NY 10011, USA
P +1 212 989 6026
F +1 212 255 3776
info@hanrahanmeyers.com
Glasser Loft - Photos: © Jordi Miralles

Ignacio Cardenal
Barcelona, Spain
Loft St. J. Malta - Photos: © Jordi Miralles

James Wagman
435 Hudson Street, Suite 403, New York,
NY 10014, USA
P +1 212 337 9649
F +1 212 337 9641
james@jameswagman.com
Sharp + Gilpin Loft - Photos: © Reto Guntli / Zapaimages

John Martin / Four Ten Architects
London, UK
P +44 898 66508
Mc. Donough Loft - Photos: © Bruno Helbingi / Zapaimages

Maria Vives, Lluís Escarmis / GCA Arquitectes

C / Valencia 289, Bajos, 08009 Barcelona, Spain
P +34 93 4761800
F +34 93 4761806
lec@gcaarq.com
www.gcaarq.com
Loft in the Old City - Photos: © Jordi Miralles

Mario Connío

Buenos Aires, Argentina
Terrace Loft - Photos: © Ricardo Labougle

Mark Grzegorczyk / MG Architects

1 Spencer Road, London SW18 2SP, UK
P +44 20 7924 3006
F +44 20 7924 2720
grzego@aol.com
www.mgarchitects.org
St. John Street Loft - Photos: © Seamus Slattery

Ogawa / Depardon Architects

137 Varick Street, Suite 404, New York, NY 10013, USA
P +1 212 627 7390
F +1 212 627 9681
ogawdep@aol.com
Greenwich Village Loft - Photos: © Kevin Chu / Jessica Paul

Ruhl Walker Architects

60K Street, Boston, MA 02127, USA
P +1 617 268 5479
F +1 617 268 5482
www.ruhlwalker.com
H / R Loft - Photos: © Jordi Miralles

Sarah Folch Estudi d'Interiorisme

Plaça. Sarrià 12, 2°1ª, 08017 Barcelona, Spain
P +34 93 280 0428
F +34 93 280 0428
sarahfolch@yahoo.es
Textile Factory - Photos: © Jordi Miralles

Sergio Sessa

Buenos Aires, Argentina
Loft in Buenos Aires - Photos: © Ricardo Labougle

Victoria Blau Architect

200 Park Avenue South, Suite 1310, New York,
NY 10003, USA
P +1 212 529 2050
F +1 212 529 2690
info@vblau.com
Duane Street Loft - Photos: © Albert Vecerka / Esto
Thirty Crosby Street Loft - Photos: © Albert Vecerka / Esto

Xavière Bouyer

Paris, France
Loft in Pigalle - Photos: © Ricardo Labougle,
Ana Cardinale

copyright © 2004 daab gmbh

published and distributed worldwide by
daab gmbh
stadtwaldgürtel 57
d - 50935 köln

t +49-221-94 10 740
f +49-221-94 10 741

mail@daab-online.de
www.daab-online.de

publisher ralf daab
rdaab@daab-online.de

art director feyyaz
mail@feyyaz.com

editorial project by loft publications
copyright © 2004 loft publications

editor Alejandro Bahamón
layout Diego González
english translation Ana Cristina G. Cañizares
french translation Jean Pierre Layre Cassou
italian translation Grazia Suffritti
german translation Martin Fischer
copy editing Raquel Vicente Durán

printed in spain
Anman Gràfiques del Vallès, Spain
www.anman.com

isbn 3-937718-11-7
d.l.: B-27622-2004